your Teacher Carefully

Compiled by John Foster

Illustrated by Robin Boyden, Mark Long, Dan Bramall,
Meg Hunt, Leo Broadley, Daron Parton, Laura Ellen Anderson,
Olga Demidova, Mark Beech, Sole Otero, Emi Ordás
and Yannick Robert

Contents

Watch your Teacher Carefully

It happened in school last week
when everything seemed fine
assembly, break, science and spelling
three twelves are four times nine.

But then I noticed my teacher
scratching the skin from her cheek
a forked tongue flicked from her lips
her nose hooked into a beak.

Her twenty arms grew longer
they ended in terrible claws
by now she was orange and yellow and green
with crunching great teeth in her jaws.

Her twenty eyes were upon me
as I ran from the room for the Head
got to his office, burst through the door
met a blood-sucking alien instead.

Somehow I got to the staffroom
the doorknob was dripping with slime
inside were seven hideous things
who thought I was dinner-time.

I made my escape through a window
just then a roaring sound
knocked me over flat on my face
as the whole school left the ground.

Powerful rockets pushed it
back into darkest space
all I have left are the nightmares
and these feathers that grow on my face.

David Harmer

The Cyclops

The Cyclops fluttered his eyelid.
He knelt down on the floor,
Looked his sweetheart in the eye
And said, 'You're the one-eye adore.'

Pam Johnson

Why did the Cyclops apply for half a television licence?

Because he only had one eye.

Why did the Cyclops give up teaching?

Because he only had one pupil.

I Wonder Why

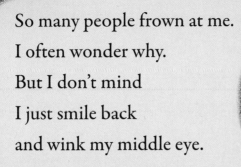

So many people frown at me.
I often wonder why.
But I don't mind
I just smile back
and wink my middle eye.

Barry Buckingham

Monster Sale!!

MONSTER SALE!! the advert said.
I'm telling you – it LIED.
There was junk galore ...
In the Super Store ...
But not ONE monster inside.

Clare Bevan

What did one ear say to the other ear?

Between us we have brains.

The Ghoul

One dark and wintry evening
When snow swirled through the air
And the wind howled like a banshee
I crept silently up the stair.

I sat in the quiet of my bedroom
And opened with bated breath
My spooky Horror Make-Up Kit
That would frighten my sister to death.

Slowly my face began to change
As I carefully applied the pack.
I laughed at my face in the mirror
But an evil stranger leered back.

Long hair sprouted wild from my forehead,
My nose was half snout, half beak,
My right eye bulged angry and bloodshot
While the left crawled over my cheek.

FAKE

My fangs hung low and broken,
My chin was cratered with sores,
The backs of my hands were mats of hair,
My fingers grew long, bird-like claws.

Heard my sister's key in the front door,
Heard her calling, 'Anyone in?'
Took a long, last look at the Thing in the glass,
Distorted and ugly as sin.

Heard her turn on the taps in the kitchen.
I crept quietly down the stair,
I heard her call out as a floorboard creaked,
'Hello, is anyone there?'

And then I released a terrible howl
As I crashed through the kitchen door.
I caught sight of a ghoul in the window pane
And passed out cold on the floor.

Gareth Owen

Jocelyn, my Dragon

My dragon's name is Jocelyn.

He's something of a joke.

For Jocelyn is very tame,

He doesn't like to maul or maim,

Or breathe a fearsome fiery flame;

He's much too smart to smoke.

And when I take him to the park

The children form a queue,

And say, 'What lovely eyes of red!'

And one by one they pat his head.

And Jocelyn is so well-bred,

He only eats a few!

Colin West

Why did the dragon keep burning his fingers?

Because his mum had told him to cover his mouth when he coughed.

Dragon Love Poem

When you smile
the room lights up

and I have to call
the fire brigade.

Roger Stevens

My Brother's Allergies

When my brother had to go into hospital,
They asked my mum
If he had any allergies.
'Yes,' she said,
'Lots. He's allergic to
Getting up in the morning,
Tidying his room,
Doing the washing-up
And listening to what I say.'

Derek Stuart

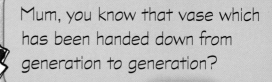

Mum, you know that vase which has been handed down from generation to generation?

Yes.

Well, this generation's dropped it.

Ten Things Mums <u>Never</u> Say

1. Keep your mouth open when you eat,
   then you'll be able to talk at the same time.

2. Jump down the stairs.
   It's quicker than walking.

3. Don't eat all your vegetables.
   You won't have room for your sweets.

4. It's too early for bed.
   Stay up and watch more television.

5. Be rude to your teachers.
   It would be dishonest to be polite.

6. By all means walk on the furniture.
   It's already badly scratched.

7. Don't brush your teeth.
   They'll only get dirty again.

8. It's not your fault that your pocket money
   only lasts for a day.

9. Wipe your feet on the sofas.
   That's what they're there for.

10. I was far worse behaved than you
    when I was young.

Steve Turner

The Disco Sheep

The disco sheep danced down the street.
He stomped his hooves to a disco bleat.

'I'm Sam the Ram. So form a queue.
I'll dance with ewe and ewe and ewe.'

'I'm the best at the Hip Hop Skip.
You're number one at the Sheep Dip Trip.'

'All you sheep wherever you are,
Shout Sam the Ram – Superbaah.'

John Coldwell

Did you know it takes three sheep to make a jumper?

I didn't know sheep could knit.

What did the polite sheep say as it stepped aside after opening the door?

After ewe.

Beware! Beryl the Budgie

She's a seed-eating, bell-beating,
Ball-bashing, mirror-smashing
Bully bird. Or haven't you heard of
Beryl the Budgie?

She wears a gold chain and a diamond ring,
And carries a pistol, tucked under her wing.
She likes tight jeans and motorbike leathers,
Unzipped to the navel to show off her feathers.

If you meet her in the street don't dare to speak
Unless she grants permission with a nod of her beak.
And never suggest that she's broken any laws
Or she'll break your neck with a twist of her claws.

She's done a few jobs driving getaway cars.
She got caught once; did time behind bars.
But now she's out and earning a packet
Running a pet shop protection racket.

She's a seed-eating, bell-beating,
Ball-bashing, mirror-smashing
Bully bird. Or haven't you heard of
Beryl the Budgie?

John Coldwell

A Flight of Fancy

I planted a packet of birdseed
In a line straight as an arrow.
I didn't get much of a crop,
Just a parrot, two ducks and a sparrow.

Colin McNaughton

What did the duck say when she bought lipstick?

Put it on my bill.

Why did the pelican refuse to pay for his meal?

Because his bill was too big.

What do snakes have on their aprons?

Hiss and Hers.

A Natural Mistake

It is a natural mistake
When playing with a rattlesnake
To grab the head and give a shake.
It's better twisted in a knot
And hung above the baby's cot.

Dave Calder

I Dreamed I Took Over

I dreamed I took over my primary school ...
I sacked the head teacher for breaking the rules,
Kept the teachers outside during break in the cold
And when they complained said, 'Do as you're told!'
I told them to stop laughing and messing about,
'The staffroom's a cesspit. Get it cleaned out!'
Several were sent home to change shirts or their ties
Or put on dull dresses of more suitable size.
I gave lots of homework, which I didn't explain;
They put up their hands and asked questions in vain.

'You should have been listening,' I said with a smile,
'Hand in tomorrow. Now line up, single file!'
I ignored their excuses that they had to go out.
'Your work must come first,' I said with a shout.
'Reports will be issued at the end of the term.
If you've not shown improvement I'll have to be firm:
It may be the thumb screws, it may be the rack ...
I'm going to wake up now – but I'll be back!'

Trevor Millum

Why Are You Late for School?

I didn't get up

because I was too tired

and I was too tired

because I went to bed late

and I went to bed late

because I had homework

and I had homework

because the teacher made me

and the teacher made me

because I didn't understand

and I didn't understand

because I wasn't listening

and I wasn't listening

because I was staring out of the window

and I was staring out of the window

because I saw a cloud.

I am late, sir,

because I saw a cloud.

Steve Turner

Teacher: I said to draw a cow eating grass, but you've only drawn a cow.

Jamil: Yes, because the cow has eaten all the grass.

Teacher: Which three words are heard most often in the classroom?

Trevor: I don't know.

Teacher: Correct.

Teacher: You copied Lisa's answers in the test, didn't you?

Alison: How did you know?

Teacher: Lisa's answer says, 'I don't know' and you've written, 'Neither do I'.

Shamyla: I didn't do my homework because I lost my memory.

Teacher: When did this start?

Shamyla: When did what start?

Parents' Evening

Hello, Mrs Spinner
About your son, Sam

First of all I must say
I'm sorry to hear about your Rottweiler
Sam says it's been poorly
Well, the number of times it's eaten Sam's homework
I'm not surprised
And then it gave Sam dog flu and he was away
On the day that Brighton played Spurs in the cup
And it was a shame that he chewed Sam's PE kit
What's that?
You don't have a Rottweiler?
You don't even have a dog?
How strange

By the way, Mrs Spinner, may I congratulate your husband
On being chosen to represent England
In the next Olympics
You must be very proud
He's a shot-putter, Sam says

And Sammy tells me you're a model
And you're in those perfume commercials

What's that?
You have to be going
You have something to say to Sammy
Well, lovely to meet you at last
Tell Sammy I'm looking forward
To seeing him tomorrow

Goodbye, Mrs Spinner
Goodbye

Roger Stevens

A teacher asked her class, 'Can people predict the future with cards?'
'My mum can,' said Ronnie.
'Really?' the teacher said.
'Yes,' said Ronnie. 'She takes one look at my report card and tells me
what will happen when my dad gets home.'

Teachers!
I Don't Understand Them

Teachers! I don't understand them.

They say:

    When you hand in your work,

    Make sure it's neat and tidy.

Then they mess it up

By scribbling illegible comments

All over it.

They say:

    Don't interrupt when I'm talking.

    Put your hand up

    And wait until I've finished.

But if they've got something to say,

They clap their hands

And stop your discussions in mid-sentence.

They say:

    Always plan your writing.

    Take your time. Think it through

    And do a rough draft.

Then they give out a practice test paper

And ask you to write a story

On a topic which doesn't interest you

In an hour.

They say:

All work and no play

Makes Jill a dull girl.

Make sure you allow yourself

Time off from your studies

To relax and enjoy yourself.

Then, when you don't hand

Your homework in on time,

Because you took their advice,

They keep you in at lunchtime.

Teachers!

I don't understand them.

John Foster

I don't think much of our teacher. She keeps asking us questions all the time. She's a teacher. She should know all the answers.

No wonder I get low marks in history. It's not my fault. The teacher keeps on asking us questions about things that happened before I was born.

Grandpa's False Teeth

When Grandpa's false teeth fell on the floor,
Before he could catch them they ran through the door.

They ran down the steps and into the street,
Where they started to gnaw at a passer-by's feet.

When Grandpa came running and begged them to stop,
They snapped at his heels and ran into a shop.

When the shopkeeper said, 'You can't come in here.
No teeth are allowed!' they just gave a sneer.

They jumped on a shelf full of sweets in their jars
And started to nibble at two chocolate bars.

The shopkeeper gave a despairing groan
And pressed nine-nine-nine on his mobile phone.

The teeth burst out laughing. 'You'll never catch us!'
Ran out of the shop and jumped onto a bus.

They said to the driver, 'Two singles to Ware.'
And, as far as I know, they're still living there.

While Grandpa sits toothless, twiddling his thumbs,
Stroking his chin and sucking his gums!

John Foster

What did one tooth
say to the other?

I'm so excited. The dentist
is taking me out today.

What did the vampire call his false teeth?

A new fangled device.

Our Teachers' Pets

The teachers in our school must think
they are working in a zoo.
Their classrooms feature many a creature
and here are just a few:

Mr Lee has a chimpanzee.
It leaps about and wriggles.
It pulls his hair and bumps his chair
and gives us all the giggles.

Mrs Drake has a ten-foot snake
inside a case of glass.
When children shout she lets it out
to quieten down the class.

Mr Matt has a vampire bat
with teeth that smile and bite.
When it's time for sums it shows its gums
and makes us get them right!

Mrs Rider wears a spider
dangling from one ear.
It does no harm, it's meant to charm
but fills us all with fear.

Mr Breeze keeps jumping fleas
in a jar on the window sill.
I wonder why his class all cry,
'Please sir, we can't sit still.'

Tony Mitton

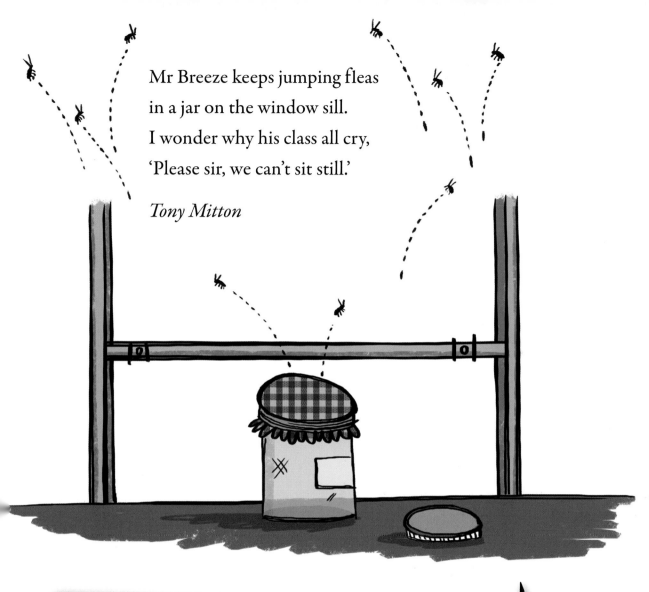

Animal School Reports

Cheetah: *A nice enough boy but not to be trusted.*

Leopard: *Has been absent a lot due to spots.*

Hyena: *Seems to think everything is a joke.*

Travellers' Tales

In Mexico
There's a TV show
Presented by a buffalo.

In Hong Kong
When they bang a gong
Everyone bursts into song.

In Nicaragua
You can watch street-dancing
Performed by a jaguar.

In Rangoon
Every afternoon a baboon
Plays tunes on a bassoon.

In Rome
People often stay at home
Playing cards with their garden gnome.

In Singapore
There's an annual tug-of-war
With a dinosaur.

And in Peru
You can practise kung fu
With a kangaroo.

John Foster

Batty Books

Polar Exploration by Ann Tartic

Where to Go in Australia by Sydney Harbour and Mel Bourne

Tropical Beach Resorts by Sandy Coves

Scuba Diving for Beginners by Coral Reef

A Week in France by Norman Dee

Eating Out in Germany *by Frank Furter*

Trips Round Chinatown by Rick Shaw

Clinking, Plinking and Plod

Clinking, Plinking and Plod one night
Sailed off in an old canoe
To visit Plod's Aunt Petunia
Who lived in a cave in Peru.

They took chocolate cake and bread to bake
And sticks of rhubarb to chew.
They took Plod's iPod and a fishing rod,
So they'd plenty of things to do.

They played Scrabble and chess
And Plod tried to guess
How much further they had to go.
But they travelled each day
In quite the wrong way,
So progress was slower than slow.

On and on they sailed, till their engine failed
On a dark and stormy night.
The current was swift and they started to drift
Without any land in sight.

The old canoe gave a shudder and shake.
It sounded as if it was going to break,
And Plod cried, 'What can we do?
It's the end of the trip. Abandon ship!
It's goodbye to this old canoe.'

With their life jackets on, they were ready to jump
When a strange vessel came into view,
And from their plight
They were rescued that night
By the crew of a wooden shoe!

John Foster

The Concise Guide for Travellers

1. For covering long distances, travel is a must.

2. Destinations are ideal places to head for.

3. By the time you get there, abroad will have moved on.

4. To avoid jet lag, travel the day before.

5. If you cross the equator go back and apologize.

6. If you meet an explorer you are lost.

Roger McGough

Postcard from School Camp

Dear Mum and Dad,

Weather's poor. Food's bad.

Teachers are grumpy. Instructors are mad.

Cramped in tent. Cold at night.

No dry clothes. Boots too tight.

Didn't like canoeing. The hiking was tough.

All in all, I've had enough.

Bye for now. MAY see you soon.

If I survive this afternoon.

Your loving son

Ben xx

P.S. Can I come again next year?

Richard Caley

Love Letter – from the Wizard to the Witch

I find your looks bewitching,
The way you stand and glare.
I love the way you shake your locks
Of tangled, matted hair.

I find your smile enchanting,
Your wicked, evil grin.
It makes me want to touch and stroke
Your gnarled and wrinkled skin.

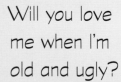

Will you love me when I'm old and ugly?

I find your face spellbinding,
The warts upon your cheek,
So hairy, black and crusty –
They make my knees go weak.

I find you so enthralling.
I love your witchy smell
Of rats and dung and sewers –
You hold me in your spell!

John Foster

Yes, dear, of course I do.

Love at First Fright

'How did you meet?' I asked
The young ghost about to be wed.
'It was during haunting practice.
I'd just put on my head.
She was floating about
And she caught my eye.
It was love at first fright,' he said.

Chris Whitby

What did the two acrobats
say when they got engaged?

We're head over heels in love.

How did the two octopuses who
were on a date swim around?

Arm in arm in arm in arm in arm in arm in arm in arm.

Holiday Print

There was a young man from Dundee
Who had a great passion to ski;
He skied with aggression
And left an impression –
The shape of himself on a tree!

Coral Rumble

Who?

I'm sure it wasn't me who spoke
While I was shinning up the oak,
So who, as I climbed up that tree,
Said, 'Get those nasty feet off me!'

Richard Edwards

Why did the tree dye its hair?

Its roots were showing.

Why is a bride out of luck on her wedding day?

She never marries the best man.

Poisoning People is Wrong

You've done it again, haven't you?
You've eaten all the cherries
And given the rest of your cake to the rabbit.

I SAY NOTHING.

And who gave the crust of the steak pie
To the dog?
Who?
I bet it was you.
He's been sick twice this morning, you know.

ALL THE MORE REASON FOR ME
NOT TO EAT IT.

I keep finding crusts all over the house.

You're supposed to eat the whole of the bread,

Not shove the bits you don't like in your pocket

And stick them in the bookcase later on.

I'd sniffed my way around

Fourteen Dickens novels

Before I found your rotten crusts.

They'd gone green.

Are you listening?

Green, they'd gone.

SO SHE'S DESTROYED MY
PENICILLIN FACTORY.
SHE HATES SCIENTISTS.

As for that cabbage:

If you'd said you didn't want it,

I wouldn't have given you so much.

You're disgusting, you are.

WELL SOMETHING WAS NEEDED
TO FILL THAT GAP AT THE BACK
OF THE SOFA.

Baked potatoes are meant
To be eaten,
Not poked about.
And don't leave the skin this time.
That's the bit with all the vitamins.

THAT'S ALSO THE BIT WITH
ALL THE MUD IF SHE'S LEFT
MY FATHER TO SCRUB THEM.

Yes, we are having rice pudding for afters.
And, yes, you do have to eat it.
You were grateful if you got rice pudding
In my day.
Things were different.

IN HER DAY IT WAS ILLEGAL
TO POISON CHILDREN.

Are you muttering something?

ME? NOT ME.

David Kitchen

Shocked!

Just look at you –
All studs and rings,
Those false nails
And that fake tattoo!
Your hair! My skirt!
Those boots! That hat!
No, Mum, you're NOT
Going out like that!

Sue Cowling

Chart Topper

My dad thinks he's a pop star.
His music's quite frenetic.
He waves his arms, rotates his hips,
I think he's just pathetic.

My dad goes on about success,
he's full of plans and schemes,
to top the charts and tour the States,
but I say – in his dreams.

And when he goes to have a shower,
Dad sings into the soap.
He's practising for his CD.
He hasn't got a hope.

My dad sings tame old ballads
and says, 'How's that? Not bad!'
My mum thinks he's terrific
but she is just as sad.

My dad wants to be discovered,
show the world that he's a whizz.
If only he'd discover
how embarrassing he is.

Alison Chisholm

About John Foster

I grew up in Carlisle and dreamed of playing football for Carlisle United, but they showed no interest in signing me. After working as a fire-fighter in Canada, I became a teacher. That's when I started to write poems and edit poetry books. I've written about 1,500 poems and compiled over 100 anthologies. None of them have been as much fun as compiling the Chucklers anthologies.

I've chuckled at the disco dancing sheep and the budgie who runs a pet shop protection racket, giggled at the ghosts who fell in love at first fright, laughed at the false teeth that ran off down the street, chortled at the boy who nearly frightened himself to death and was reminded of my dad's out of tune singing by 'Chart Topper'.